CNF
741.2

D0508030

WATERFORD CITY AND COUNTY
WITHDRAWN
LIBRARIES

Waterford City and County
Libraries

3, 2, 1...

DRAW!

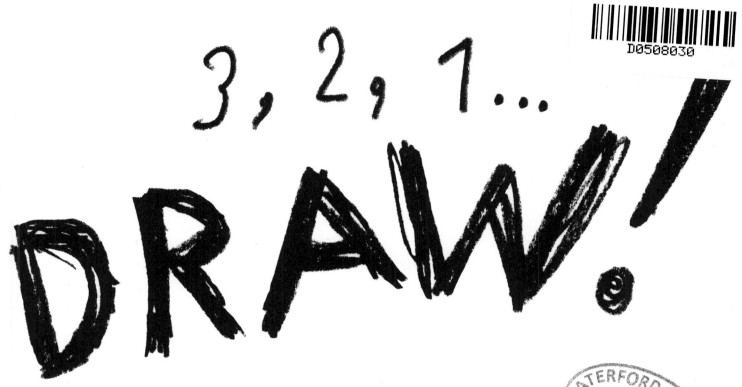

SERGE BLOCH

WATERFORD CITY AND COUNTY WITHDRAWN LIBRARIES

What is this aubergine saying?

How many other creatures are hiding in Asparagus Forest?

Can you name these pan-bots?

Create your own pan-vention.

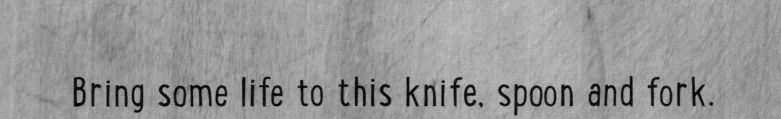
Bring some life to this knife, spoon and fork.

A cupful of love...

What's the story here?

Add some snails to this trail.

Create your own big cheese.

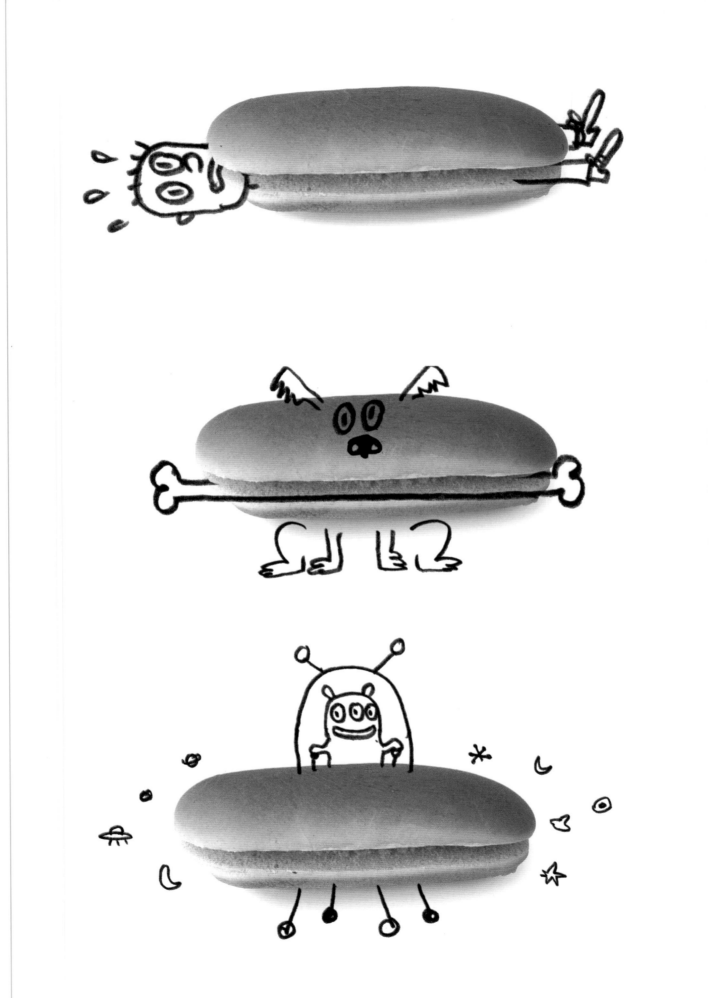

Who (or what) is ready to roll?

Who else is in the hot seat?

What other telephone transformations are taking place?

Who is making a spectacle of themselves?

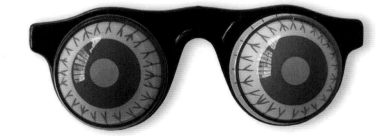

Design your own tower blocks.

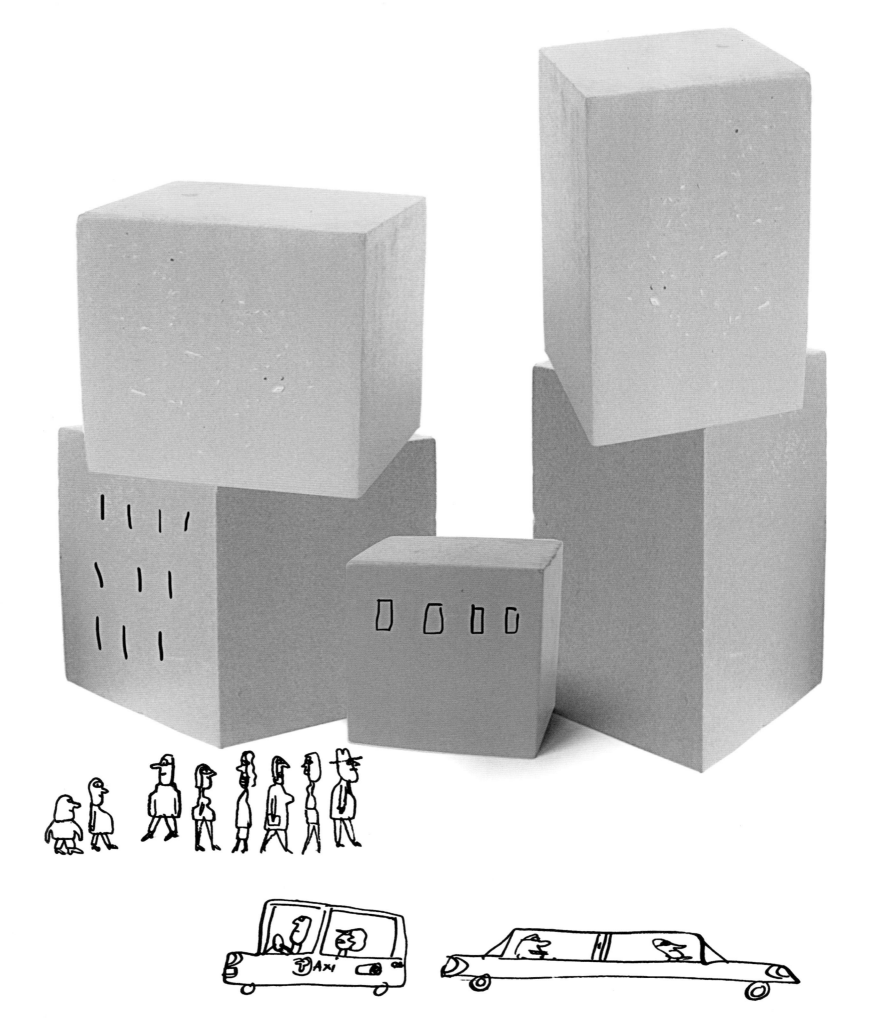

Dear Mummy
Love
xoxo

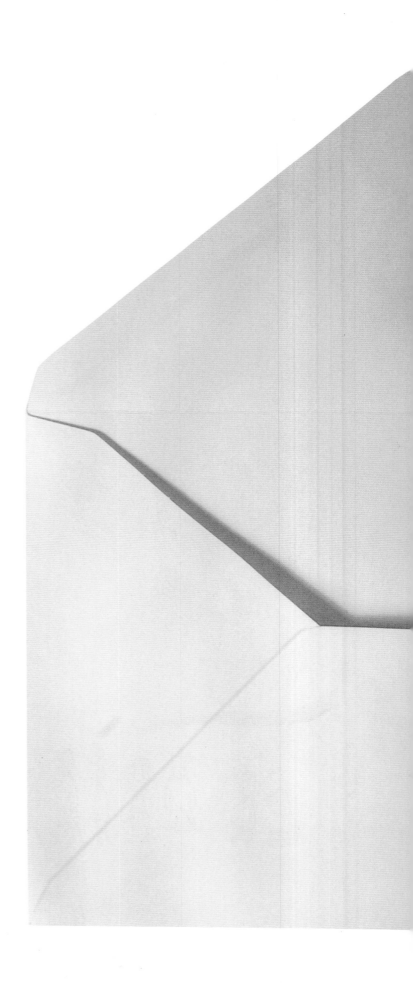

What message would you like to send?

Who is in a jam?

What other characters are getting keyed up?

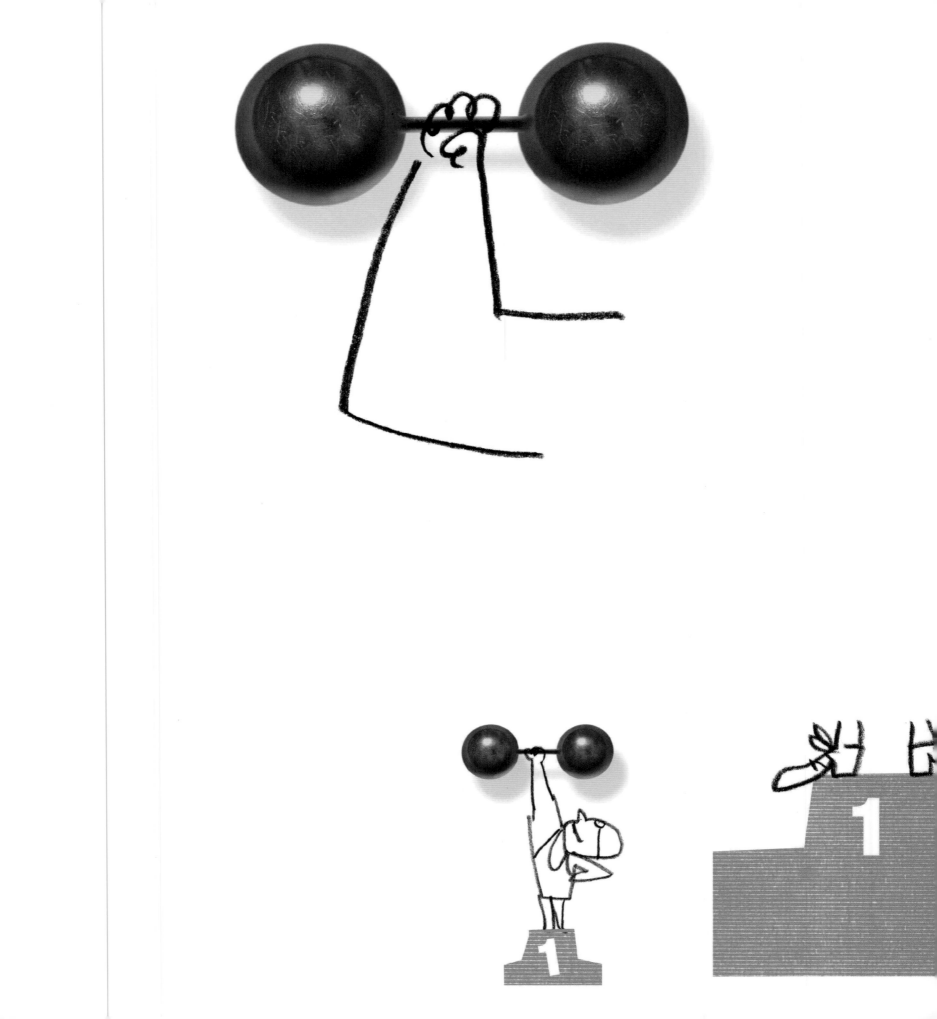

Who is the strongest of them all?

TRANSFORM YOUR BEDROOM

Who is under each of these hats?

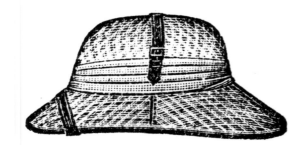

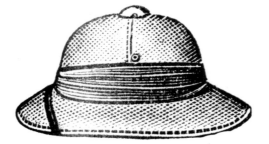

Give each bear a belly.

Who else is keeping an eye on things?

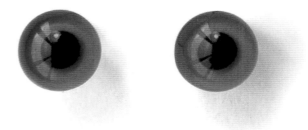

What has set the alarm bells ringing?

Create some covers.

W. SHEKSPAR
HOMLET

PINGUEN
CLASSIC

Who else has slipped into a slipper?

What is lurking among these lamps?

Who will not be brushed aside?

Draw some more seafarer's stories.

What is flying through these clouds of cotton?

Who's a lucky duck?

What is on tap here?

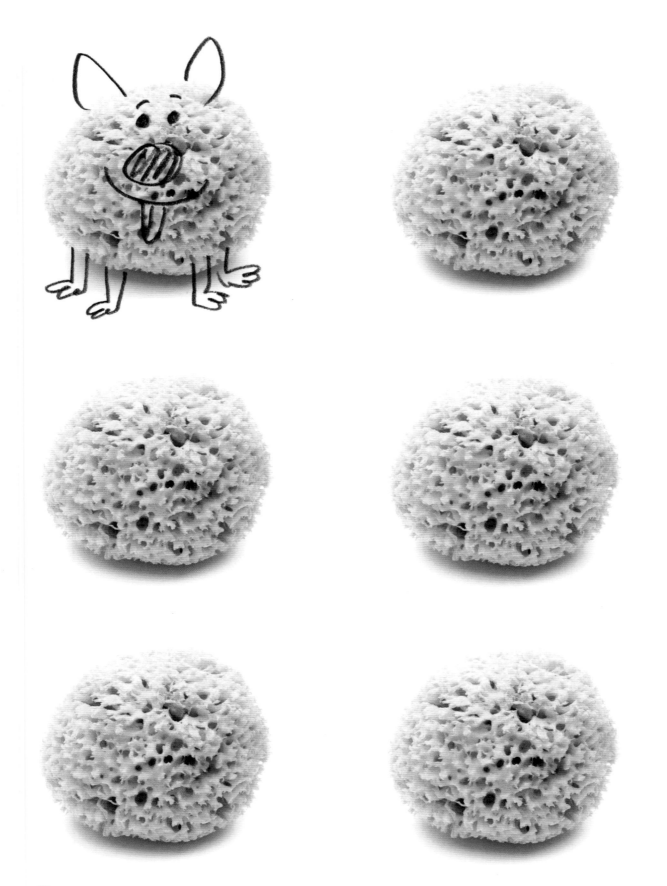

Draw some more squeaky-clean creatures.

Mirror, mirror, on the wall, can you fill these pictures, all?

Who set the roll rolling?

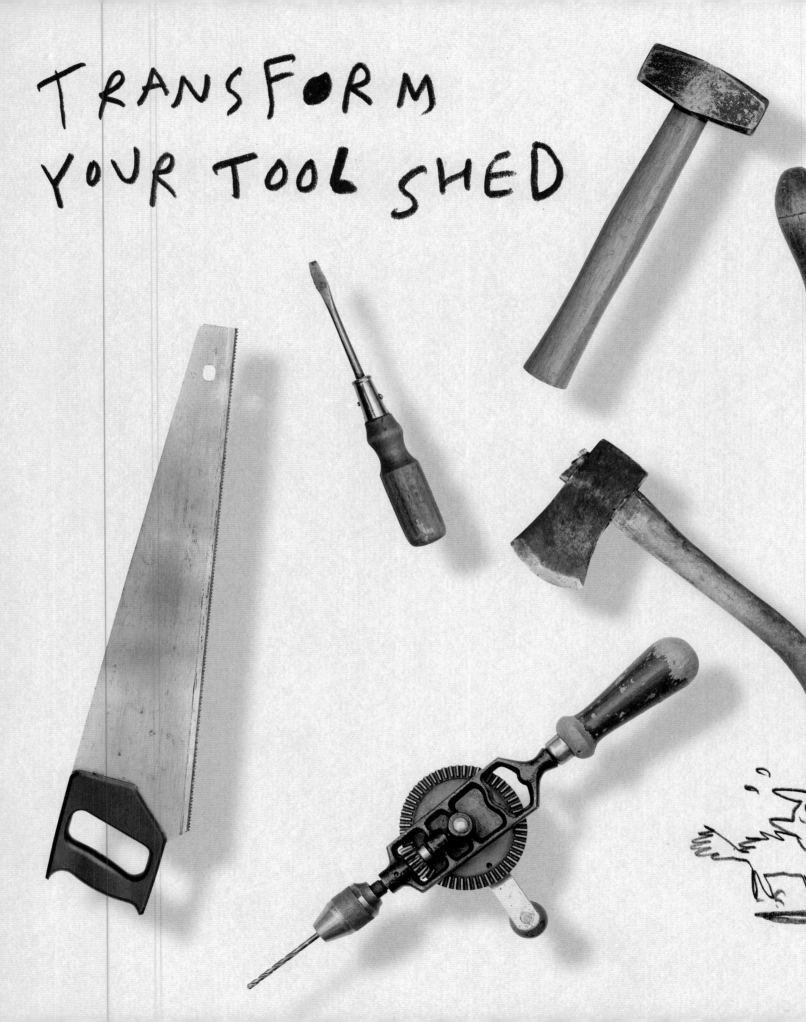

TRANSFORM
YOUR TOOL SHED

Bring your own inventions to light.

Who – or what – is feeling red-faced?

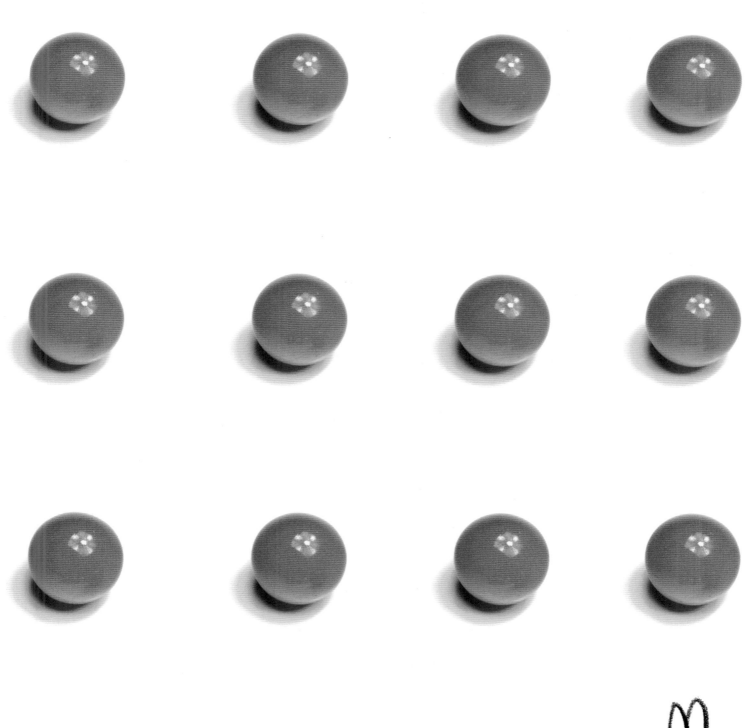

FIRE FIRE!

Who else is coming to the rescue?

Who is pulling on this string?

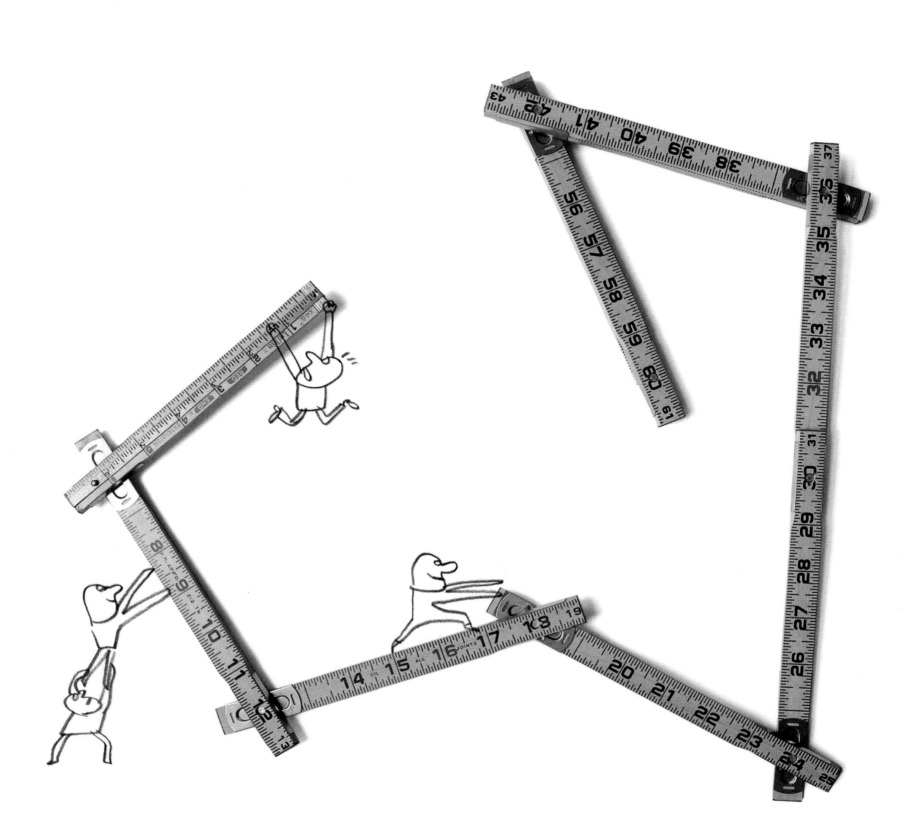

Who is ruling the roost?

Who is doing
the spadework here?

TRANSFORM YOUR GARDEN

Add some feathered
friends hiding in
these branches.

Who else is having a prickly conversation?

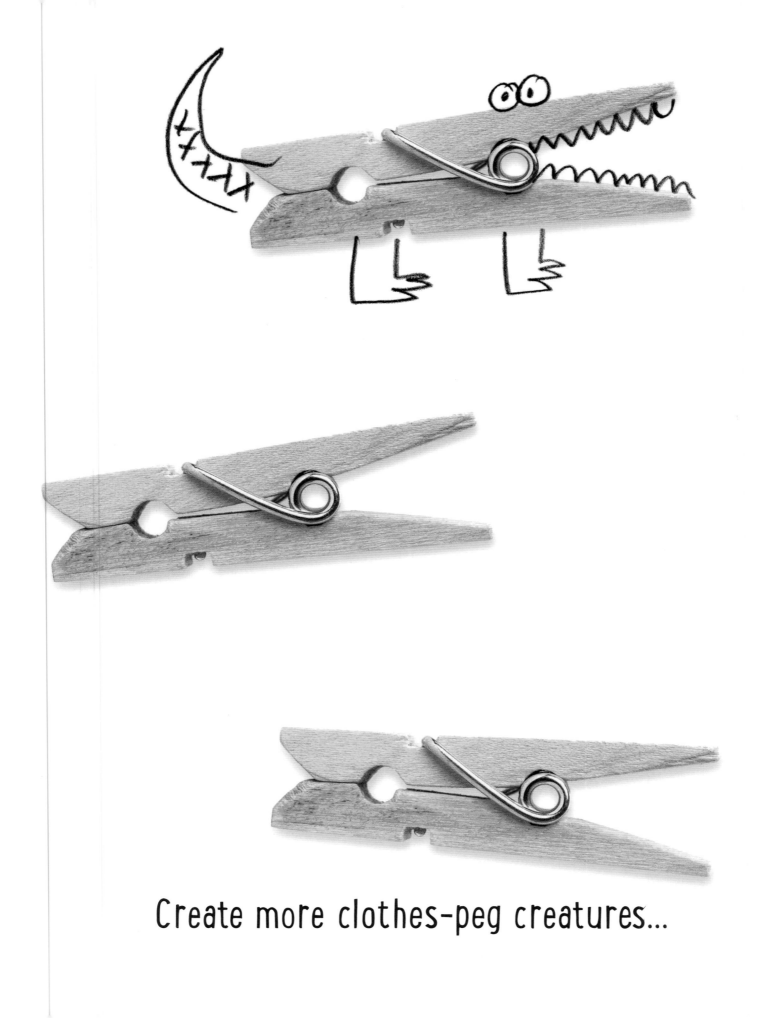

Create more clothes-peg creatures...

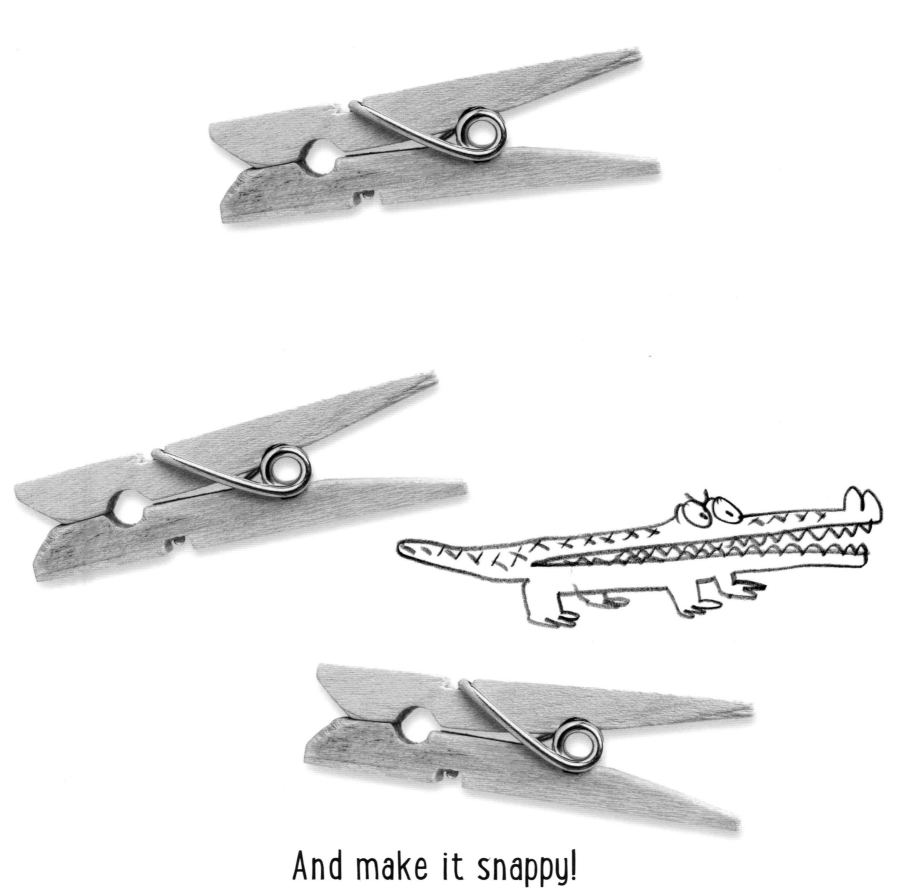

And make it snappy!

Add some
flower power.

Create a crew of conker-ers!

Who is ready to fly the nest?

Create your own
can of worms.

Wide Eyed Editions
www.wideeyededitions.com

3,2,1... Draw! copyright © Aurum Press Ltd 2016
Illustrations copyright © Serge Bloch 2016

First published in Great Britain in 2016 by
Wide Eyed Editions, an imprint of Aurum Press,
74–77 White Lion Street, London N1 9PF
www.aurumpress.co.uk

All rights reserved

No part of this publication may be reproduced, stored in a retrieval system, or transmitted,
in any form, or by any means, electrical, mechanical, photocopying, recording or otherwise
without the prior written permission of the publisher or a licence permitting restricted copying.
In the United Kingdom such licences are issued by the Copyright Licensing Agency,
Saffron House, 6-10 Kirby Street, London EC1N 8TS.

A catalogue record for this book is available from the British Library.

ISBN 978-1-84780-724-3

The illustrations were created with mixed media
Set in Lunchbox

Designed by Nicola Price
Edited by Jenny Broom
Published by Rachel Williams

Printed in November 2015 in Shenzhen, Guangdong, China

1 3 5 7 9 8 6 4 2